This book is the property of:

Name: _____

Surname: _____

Address: _____

_____

School: _____

Madiba
THE RAINBOW MAN

DEDICATION

This book I dedicate to Brent and Tarra,
my children who inspired me to write this story.

And to my late mother, Rachel,
whom I will always love and cherish.

Also to President Nelson Mandela and all those
who contributed in the struggle to give us
the freedom and joy we share today.

BENEFITING THE
Nelson Mandela
CHILDREN'S FUND

Asjen cc, 205 Main Road, Wynberg

© Lionel John Maxim 1997

First published 1997

ISBN 0 620 21765 0

Set in 12 on 18 point Galliard by Left Justified cc
Reproduction by Castle Graphics
Imagesetting by Tone Graphics
Printed by National Book Printers, Drukkery Street, Goodwood, Cape Town

BIBLIOGRAPHY

In writing this book the following sources were used for research and inspiration:

Long Walk to Freedom by Nelson Mandela, published by MacDonald Purnell

Long Walk to Freedom (illustrated version) by Nelson Mandela, published by Little,
    Brown and Company

Higher Than Hope by F. Meer, published by Penguin Books

Robben Island – Symbol of Resistance by Barbara Hutton, published by Sached Books

Nelson Mandela: The Struggle is My Life (Fourth Edition), published by David Philip and
    Pathfinder

SPECIAL THANKS TO:

Felicia Siebritz at the Mayibuye Centre for all the research material made available to me.
My friend Aslam Gierdien for your support of this project.
Clive Barrows for your hours given at all times.

Janis Chapman (Nelson Mandela Children's Fund)
Dream Furnishers staff
Prof. Jakes Gerwel (Secretary-General of the President's office)
Ali Gierdien (President Cape Chamber of Commerce)
Dr H.E. Joosub (CEO Rublan Investments)
Ahmed Kathrada (Advisor to President Nelson Mandela)
Jeremy Ractliffe (Nelson Mandela Children's Fund)
Franklin Sonn (S.A. Ambassador to U.S.A.)
Gene Swanepoel (Maskew Miller Longman)
Archbishop Desmond Tutu (Chairperson Truth and Reconciliation Commission)
Shanaaz van der Schyff (University of the Western Cape)
Nicky van Driel (Language editor)
Peter J. Volkwyn

And finally my sisters, Jenny, Marlene and Nolene,
for your support and love that has kept me going.

Nelson Mandela
CHILDREN'S FUND

Madiba the Rainbow Man

This book enables children to readily identify and be involved with Nelson Mandela's incredible adventure from a small country village to the highest Office of State, with much hardship in the years between – borne with unique courage and unshakeable determination to create a free and just South Africa.

We hope that it will inspire young people to become involved in shaping a better world, for themselves and their peers.

President Mandela has said that, in creating a new South Africa our children must be one of our highest priorities. They are the foundations on which our future is being built. It was to lend urgency to the task that he launched the Children's Fund so that all people who wished to make their own direct contribution including himself, could do so and thereby alleviate the terrible plight of many children in our communities and help them prepare for a brighter tomorrow.

In creating this book for children, first-time author Lionel Maxim and his friend, businessman Aslam Gierdien have shown much determination and sustained effort to ensure that at least 20% of the book price, in bookstores, flows to the Nelson Mandela Children's Fund as a donation from all those who purchase the book.

This is a wonderful example of how individuals can enable people from all walks of life to join them in making a significant contribution towards aiding children at risk in our country.

We thank them and you, the Reader, for investing in the future of our Rainbow Nation.

JEREMY RACTLIFFE, CHIEF EXECUTIVE TRUSTEE

Fundraising Number: 011 013 370 008   E-mail: nmcf@mail.icon.co.za
Web address: http://www.web.co.za/mandela/children
P O Box 797 , Highlands North, 2037   33 Scott Street, Waverley, 2090.
Telefax: (+27 11) 786 917 Tel: (+27 11) 786 9140

A special thanks goes to the following companies
who assisted in this noble venture
"Madiba, The Rainbow Man"

Auto Atlantic
V&A Waterfront

Dream Furnishers

Madiba

THE RAINBOW MAN

by
Lionel J Maxim

Illustrations by
Rassie Erasmus

THE STORY OF NELSON MANDELA — CHILDREN'S VERSION

PUBLISHED BY ASJEN CC

Foreword

I am delighted to have the honour of writing a foreword to this important book. It is important because it is written for our children and our children's children. They are the future leaders of our beloved country and they should understand the story of perhaps the greatest South African who has ever lived.

The story of Nelson Mandela will be in every history book but Lionel Maxim gives young people not a figure in history, but a real, live person. A person who loves his family, who loves his country and its people passionately and, above all, who has enormous courage and humanity. Madiba's life has been full of drama, his biography makes exciting reading. In addition, the outstanding illustrations by Rassie Erasmus are a real treat which place the reader right in the life and times of the period.

Young people need heroes and it is tremendously important that they realise that heroes were children once. They are ordinary people who often come from poor and humble homes. What makes them heroes are their dreams and a belief that, however impossible it may seem, they can make their dreams come true and not only for themselves but for others too, even a whole country.

Children often play the game "When I grow up I want to be a … driver, teacher, doctor etc." After reading this book I hope that many will say, "When I grow up I want to be a great leader like Nelson Mandela." If they can do so with some understanding of the commitment, sacrifices and courage required to make the world a better place, Lionel Maxim will have achieved much and given South Africa a better chance of being the great nation we have the potential to become.

DESMOND TUTU
ARCHBISHOP EMERITUS

Contents

One

The Chief

In a tiny village called Mveso, there once lived a Thembu tribe and their chief. The tribe belonged to the Xhosa nation, and their village Mveso was built on the banks of the Mbashe River in a place called the Transkei. Their chief's name was Gadla Henry Mphakanyisa. Chief Gadla, as he was known to all the villagers, was a respected and important man for he was an advisor to the king of the Thembu tribe. Chief Gadla had four wives and thirteen children. He was both feared and loved by the children of the village as he was a strict man.

As a chief, Chief Gadla had to travel between the villages to settle arguments between farmers over lost or stolen cattle. When the time came for the king to select a successor to the throne, he summoned Chief Gadla to help him. The king had so much respect for Chief Gadla's wisdom that he immediately accepted his suggestion that the king's son, Jongitaba, should be chosen as successor. The future king promised Chief Gadla that he would repay him one day. We shall find out all about this later in this story.

One day, a messenger arrived at Chief Gadla's village with an urgent message from the white magistrate. Chief Gadla was summoned to settle a complaint someone had laid against him. The chief was angry. Why did the magistrate not show him the respect he deserved as a tribal leader? He sent away the messenger with a harsh message to the magistrate. This made the magistrate angry. He felt insulted by the black man's words. The magistrate decided to punish the chief. He took away his title, most of his

1

cattle and his land. Chief Gadla became a poor man who could no longer afford to support his large family. Each of his four wives moved with her children to different villages, where family and friends helped to clothe and feed them.

One of Chief Gadla's sons was called Rolihlahla Mandela. The name "Rolihlahla" means "pulling the branch of the tree" or "trouble-maker". Rolihlahla Mandela moved with his mother, Nosekeni Fanny, to a village north of the Mbashe River. This village is called Qunu. It was larger than Mveso, with more huts and wide open fields. Rolihlahla was young and unaware of the problems that faced his family. But at least he could notice that they had moved to a very beautiful place. The lush green valleys and crystal clear streams were overlooked by green hills. It is here, in the green village of Qunu, where our story begins.

Two

Growing up

Qunu was home to mostly women and children. The men worked on faraway farms and on mines in the big cities. They came home only twice a year, to plough the land. Most of the work in the village was done by the women and children. By the time Rolihlahla was five years old, he had already become a herdboy. He was happy to spend time in the fields which he loved so much.

Soon he learnt to swim in the clear cold streams and to catch fish with twine. He loved the sweet warm milk from the udders of the cows. While they were looking after the cattle, he and the other herdboys played together. Stickfighting was his favourite game. This game is part of African tradition, and every young boy learns to stickfight. Rolihlahla dreamt of one day being the best stickfighter ever.

At night, after the cattle were returned to the kraal, his mother would have supper prepared in one of their three huts. In the village most families had three huts: one to store food in, another to cook in and a third one to sleep in. Although they had less than before, Rolihlahla's family always had enough to eat and shared freely with others. The last part of the evening came after supper, at the fire. Here Rolihlahla heard tales of great Xhosa warriors and big battles won by kings of various tribes. The children of the village mimicked actions and performed war cries while everybody around the fire enjoyed the wonderful stories. Sometimes a lie or two helped to keep everyone listening and interested. When the elders visited the village from time to time, they would quickly gather just to hear a new tale, or an old one with new additions.

Most people in the village wore tribal clothes. Rolihlahla was usually dressed in a blanket which was tied to his waist, even when they attended Sunday school. His mother was a Christian. Although Rolihlahla's father did not accept the Christian ways and believed in his ancestors and their gods, he never stopped them from going to the small local church.

One day as Rolihlahla returned from the field he saw his mother and George Mbekela having a chat. Years ago Mr Mbekela helped to get Rolihlahla baptised in church. Old Mr Mbekela used to be a teacher and everyone in the village respected him. As Rolihlahla came closer, he heard Mr Mbekela say, "Your son is very clever. He should go to school." Rolihlahla's mother just smiled. Rolihlahla anxiously awaited his father's visit, wondering whether he would receive a good education.

Three

Going to school

For one week of every month, the chief came to stay with Rolihlahla and his mother. He stayed for only a week, since he also had to spend time with his other wives and children. Rolihlahla was always happy to see his father. He looked forward to Chief Gadla's visits. When it was time for the next visit, Rolihlahla was very excited. He knew that his mother would ask his father's permission to send him to school. Chief Gadla had a great respect for Mr Mbekela whom he knew well.

Out in the field Rolihlahla could think of nothing else but going to school. In his imagination he pictured being able to read and write. His friends called him to come and play, but he heard nothing. He was in a world of his own. Then at last his father arrived and Rolihlala's mother called him to the hut. When the chief saw him, he gave a warm smile and hugged Rolihlahla as he always did. "My son," he said, "I believe you are such a clever fellow. You have done this family proud. Your mother has asked me to allow you to go to school and I have agreed." Rolihlahla beamed with joy and could not thank his father enough.

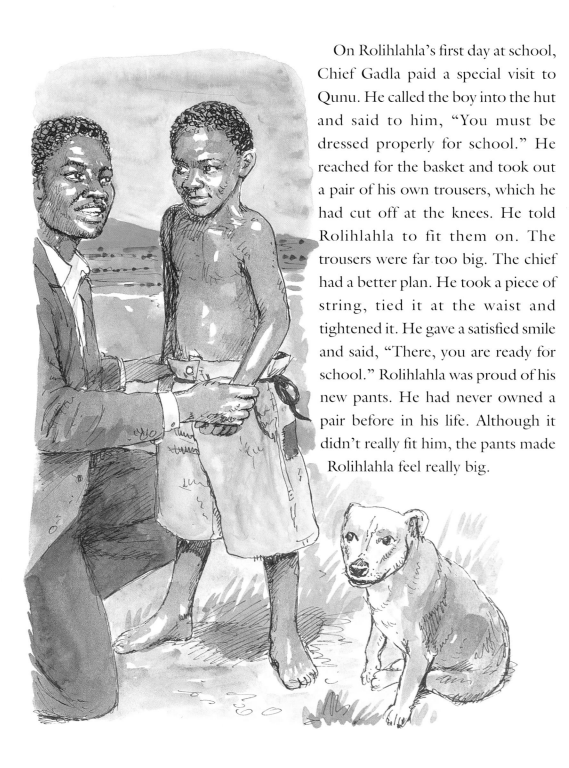

On Rolihlahla's first day at school, Chief Gadla paid a special visit to Qunu. He called the boy into the hut and said to him, "You must be dressed properly for school." He reached for the basket and took out a pair of his own trousers, which he had cut off at the knees. He told Rolihlahla to fit them on. The trousers were far too big. The chief had a better plan. He took a piece of string, tied it at the waist and tightened it. He gave a satisfied smile and said, "There, you are ready for school." Rolihlahla was proud of his new pants. He had never owned a pair before in his life. Although it didn't really fit him, the pants made Rolihlahla feel really big.

The school was on the other side of the hill at Qunu. Rolihlahla enjoyed the long walk through the fields to school every day. The school was a one-roomed long hut. On their first day at school each new child was given a Christian name. The name that Miss Mdigane chose for Rolihlahla was Nelson. Rolihlahla was very proud of his new English name, and he liked the school. He soon learnt to read and write and he made new friends.

Nelson could think of no better place than his school and village. He loved the open fields and green valleys. Every evening after his homework he would help his mother with house chores. Later he would sit around the fire and listen to tales told by the elders. Some nights Nelson and his friends would play hide and seek and at other times he would show the children new games he had learnt at school.

Four years after Nelson started school he could read, write and do arithmetic. Most children in the village could not do these things.

Four

Leaving Qunu

Nelson was now nine years old. Everybody in the village liked him. He thought he would live in Qunu forever. Little did he know how soon that would change.

One night after herding the sheep into the kraal, he heard strange voices coming from the hut he shared with his mother. The boy was shocked by what he saw there. His father was lying on the sleeping mat, and Nelson could hear that something was wrong. His father was coughing and groaning terribly. Nelson was puzzled. What was the chief doing here? They expected him only the following week.

Nelson watched his father become weaker each day. He felt helpless and sad at the thought of losing him. The people of the village helped his mother attend to his sick father and Chief Gadla's youngest wife also came to help.

Everybody was dismayed when the chief called for his pipe one evening. They told him it would be bad for him to smoke, but he kept on calling for it, so they reluctantly gave it to him. He took a few puffs and became calm, and with his pipe still lit, he died peacefully. The funeral was a sad occasion. Many people came from different villages to show their respect.

Soon after the funeral Nelson's mother told him he would have to leave Qunu. Nelson accepted her decision, and started to prepare for his journey to the unknown. He was sad to leave as the village and school was a big part of his life. He felt that no matter where he went, his heart would always be in Qunu.

Nelson's mother woke him early one morning. He packed his few belongings and they set off on foot. As they climbed the hill overlooking Qunu, Nelson turned to take a last look at the village and the three huts he loved so much. He could see the cattle moving towards the fields and smoke rising up into the clear blue skies. Nelson gave a sigh. He turned and followed his mother.

They walked in silence for most of the day. They crossed streams and walked along rocky dirt roads. They passed smaller villages. All the time they walked in a westwardly direction.

It was just before sunset when they reached their destination at the bottom of a shallow valley. Nelson was exhausted yet he could not help noticing how beautiful the place before him was. It had a big and grand house standing in the shade of two gum trees. He stared at the well-kept maize fields and apple and peach trees. A church stood close to the house. Nelson realised that someone important lived here. He would soon learn that this was the palace of the chief of the Thembu tribe, and also a new home for him.

Five

The Regent's palace

Nelson then heard that regent Jongintaba had offered to become his guardian after his father's death. This was the regent's way of showing his gratitude to Nelson's father for choosing him as a successor to the kingdom, many years ago.

As Nelson and his mother entered the kraal and walked toward the big white house, a car approached the gates. As the car passed, some men sitting in the shade jumped to their feet shouting, "Hail Jongintaba!"

When the car stopped a short, well-dressed man stepped out. He shook hands with the men who sat beneath the tree. With a warm smile and open arms, he turned to Nelson and his mother and said, "Welcome to your new home, my son."

Nelson's mother stayed a few days before she had to return to Qunu. Their farewell was not sad. Before she left, she called Nelson aside and gave him a hug. "Be brave my, boy," she said.

Nelson kept busy by exploring his new surroundings. He attended school in the rondavel next door to the palace. As before, Nelson was a good student. After school he helped as a ploughboy, a wagon guide and a shepherd. He also rode horses. The palace was the best place in the world to him and food was plentiful. At night the Thembu maidens would sometimes sing to the regent. Nelson loved dancing to their delightful tunes.

A friendship blossomed between Nelson and the regent's son, Justice. They were like brothers. Justice was the regent's only son and four years older than Nelson. Justice was a fine sportsman and attended Clarkebury, the only black boarding school in the area.

When Justice was not at home, Nelson would do odd jobs for the regent. He liked to iron the regent's suits and took great pride in his work. The regent loved Nelson like a son. He fondly gave him the nickname Tatumkhulu, which means old man.

Now and then, Nelson also got up to some mischief. One Sunday he dodged church service to fight with boys from another village. The regent

was a strict man and gave Nelson a hiding as punishment. Nelson never missed another Sunday service. Another day, the boy crawled into the garden of the priest and stole some mealies. He made a fire on which he roasted the mealies. A young girl saw him and reported the matter to the regent's wife. Nelson received a good scolding. He promised never to take anything that did not belong to him ever again.

Then the time came for Nelson to become a young man in the Xhosa tradition. This was all arranged by the elders of the village. The chosen young men stayed in the veld after they were circumcised. On their return from the veld they were met by the villagers. A big feast was held to celebrate the birth of the young men and presents were given to them. The regent gave Justice a herd of cattle. Nelson received a smaller herd. He felt overjoyed. Never in his life had he ever owned anything. After the feast the regent told Nelson more good news. He was to attend Clarkebury School with Justice.

Six

Years of study

On the day of Nelson's departure to Clarkebury School, the regent himself drove him across the Mbashe River. Nelson had never crossed this big river before. He was a young man entering a new world. His life would never be the same again.

Upon arrival the regent took Nelson to the principal's office. Reverend Harris knew the regent well. The regent saw Reverend Harris as a white Thembu, the only white man who understood and loved the Thembu people. After the regent told Nelson what was expected of him, he gave him one pound. It was the largest amount of money Nelson had ever received. The regent then said good-bye.

Reverend Harris was strict. Everyone respected him. Nelson worked hard and completed his studies in two years. Afterwards, he joined Justice in Healdtown College, then the largest African school in southern Africa. Many important people visited the school. Nelson did not study on Sundays, which was the day on which they had lunch in the main hall with the female students. This he never liked as he didn't know how to eat with a knife and fork. Many Sundays Nelson left the table hungry as he could not get the food to stay on his fork. Feeling embarrassed, Nelson worried about the girls laughing at him.

After completing his schooling the regent sent Nelson to study at the University of Fort Hare, in the town of Alice. Nelson received his first suit from the regent. Justice played the fool too much, and as a result he had to stay behind to complete his schooling.

Nelson was never lonely at Fort Hare, as some of his school friends joined him there. He studied hard and was well liked by everyone. He had an older nephew, K.D. Matanzima, who took him under his wing and even shared his pocket money with him. This made Nelson feel more at home. He attended student meetings where he met Oliver Tambo. This friendship became an important part of his life. Many years later, they would both become lawyers and open a law firm together.

Nelson returned home for the summer holidays. He was happy to see the regent and his family again. Justice had left school and was staying in Cape Town. The palace was busy as usual with people coming and going at all times. Nelson helped the regent carry out his daily tasks. He resumed his normal duties as a herdboy. One morning, the regent called Justice and Nelson to his palace, where he announced his plans for the two young men. Nelson and Justice were to be married to two young ladies whom the regent had chosen for them. Nelson was shocked but could not say anything. It was the custom and one could not argue against the wishes of the regent. The marriage was to take place as soon as the regent returned from a two-day trip.

Seven

Running away

Neither Justice nor Nelson wished to marry. "We have to run away," said Justice in a scared and squeaky voice. Nelson suggested they talk to the regent's wife. Maybe she could convince the regent to cancel the wedding. However, the regent's wife said she could not interfere with the custom. She tried to console them, saying, "After all, they are two lovely girls and they come from fine families." The only plan left was to run away as soon as possible. Nelson thought they should wait for the regent to leave on his trip. This would give them two days to get to Johannesburg.

They spent all day in the maize field watching the regent prepare for his trip, as they planned and prepared for theirs. Once the regent's car had disappeared over the hill they ran to pack, fitting what they both had in one suitcase. The regent returned almost immediately to fetch something he had forgotten. They had to quickly hide in the field behind the main house. They heard him ask his wife, "Have you seen the boys today?"

She told him not to worry. "They must be out in the field somewhere," she said. At last he left.

Nelson and Justice had little money so they decided to trade two of the regent's prize oxen. The trader thought they were sent by the regent and gave them a good price. Nelson and Justice felt bad about this but knew they had no choice. They used this money to hire a car to take them to the station. There Nelson and Justice were refused tickets. The regent had been there before to tell the ticket-office not to sell tickets to either Justice or Nelson. He suspected they might try to run away. They jumped back into the car and begged the driver to take them to the next station. They finally boarded a train and started their journey.

It was early afternoon when they reached Queenstown. Nelson accompanied Justice to see his uncle who was the chief in Queenstown. The chief was glad to see them. He believed their story about being on an errand for the regent, and took them to the local white magistrate to get them travel papers. In those days black people were not allowed to travel without documents, and could be arrested and jailed if they did not have them.

But then their luck started running out. The magistrate in Queenstown decided to telephone his friend who was the magistrate in Umtata, telling him about the favour he was doing for the regent. As it so happened the regent was visiting the magistrate in Umtata at that very time. The Queenstown magistrate was furious when he realised that Nelson and Justice had been telling him a pack of lies. Justice's uncle gave both young men a scolding and apologised to the magistrate. Nelson tried to defend their actions to the magistrate. He tried to reason with him but they were thrown out of the magistrate's office, without the travel papers. Nelson and Justice felt hurt and embarrassed. They roamed the streets of Queenstown for a short while, although it seemed like hours. Justice remembered an old friend he knew and decided to pay him a visit.

Sidney was overjoyed to see Justice and quickly put them at ease. He told them of someone who would be going to Johannesburg the following day. This news brought broad smiles to their faces. They made their way to Sidney's work to meet this person.

The old white lady was happy to have passengers to share the petrol cost. This drained the young men's pockets, but they had to get to Johannesburg. After spending the night with Sidney they departed early the next morning. The road was long and hot as they travelled through the countryside, leaving the Transkei behind them.

Nelson felt tired as they passed over one hill after the other, into the growing darkness. He never thought Johannesburg was so far away. He sat up straight as something caught his attention. Thousands of lights were flickering in the distance. It looked as if all the stars had fallen from the night sky and landed on the ground. It was indeed Johannesburg, the place they also called Egoli, the city of gold.

Eight

City of Gold

Thousands of cars drove on the city roads. Nelson was dumbstruck by the picture unfolding before his eyes. Huge glamorous billboards were on the side of the road advertising cooldrinks, soap and candy. Justice was not so dazzled by all of this, as he had stayed in Cape Town and had seen a big city before. The old lady knew the city and soon they entered an area with big and beautiful houses. Even the smallest house was five times the size of the regent's palace back home.

They entered the driveway of one of these huge homes. The old lady told Justice and Nelson to stay over, as it was very dangerous in the city at night. As they lay awake in a small shed at the back of the garden they listened to the sounds of the city. Nelson wondered what the future had in store for him. Very tired, he soon fell asleep. He was excited to be in the city and the hard floor felt like a soft bed to him.

Crown Mines was busy when they arrived there at the break of day. Strange noises were coming from all directions as the machines clattered along. They went to the office of the mine foreman, a Mr Piliso, and introduced themselves. Nelson soon realised how respected the regent was and the power he held. Mr Piliso was a tough-looking man. He told Justice how honoured he felt to give the regent's son a job. However, the regent had not mentioned anything about Nelson. Justice quickly told him that a letter was on its way from the regent in which he explained everything. Mr Piliso accepted their story and without saying another word gave both of them jobs.

They were both happy. Nelson got a job as a watchman, while Justice worked in the office of the mine. Soon, Nelson and Justice discovered that being a regent's son was very profitable. Following a tribal tradition, Justice was immediately showered with gifts and money, as a token of respect shown to the regent's son. This was much to the delight of Justice and Nelson, who had almost no money when they arrived. Feeling like rich men they shared their new-found fortune between them.

Their dream was shattered when Mr Piliso called them to his office. He showed them a telegram he had just received from the regent. It read:

Without batting an eyelid, Mr Piliso fired them. He told them to go home immediately.

Nelson and Justice thought about their actions. They felt bad about the many lies they had told. They decided to find new jobs and a new place to stay. Nelson returned to the mine to fetch their suitcase. He was hoping not to run into Mr Piliso again.

But more bad luck was to follow. As he walked towards the mine gates, a friend patted Nelson on the shoulder. "Can I help you carry your case? It is the least I can do," he said, looking sorry for Nelson. Nelson agreed. The friend walked a short distance ahead of him. The mine watchman stopped the friend to search the case. The friend told the watchman that he was stupid to do this. This made the watchman very angry, so he looked through the case again. This time he found a gun. Nelson had not told anyone about this dangerous weapon he carried in his case. The watchman blew his whistle, calling the police. The worried and shocked friend was taken to the police station. Nelson stood watching, without saying anything. This was a real test. Would Nelson be his old, honest self again?

Nelson went to the police to confess that the gun was his. He had brought it to protect himself against the city gangsters as he was only a country boy. Nelson explained further that the gun used to belong to his father. The friend was released. The next day the magistrate gave Nelson a warning and a small fine before he sent him on his way.

Justice soon got a job as a clerk on the mines. Nelson turned to his cousin, Garlick, for a place to stay. Garlick was friendly and helpful to Nelson, who was getting worried about his life in the city. Things were not going smoothly at all. Yet his dream still was to stay and become a lawyer there.

Garlick decided to help. The next day, they took an early train into the city. Garlick had a friend in the city who had his own business and knew lots of important people. As they entered the tidy office in Market Street, Nelson could feel his heart skip a beat. He had felt the same way only once before, when he had seen the regent's palace for the first time in his boyhood days.

A beautiful typist greeted Nelson and Garlick with a smile. Nelson had never seen a black typist before. She announced their arrival to her boss in the other office and waved them through. As he entered Nelson was once again taken aback. Garlick introduced him to his well-dressed friend.

"Walter Sisulu is my name," said the successful-looking young man, as he introduced himself with a firm and warm handshake. Walter found Nelson a job with a friend of his, a white lawyer. Nelson was happy to work in the big city. He started his new life in all eagerness and worked hard to please the firm and himself.

Johannesburg was a fast city for a country boy like Nelson. Around him there were smart suits, fancy cars and glitter. But he was not to be fooled by all of this.

Nine

Freedom for all

During the day Nelson worked hard at his job. At night he would study by candlelight. Nelson moved from Garlick's already overcrowded house and went to stay with Reverend Mabutho for a short while. He later found a single tin shack room of his own, in the backyard of a good family. It was not much but Nelson was happy to be on his own at last. Mr Xhoma, his landlord, was one of the few blacks allowed to own their own homes.

At work Nelson made a new friend by the name of Gaur, who took Nelson under his wing and showed him around. Gaur introduced him to more friends and important people. As a country boy everything was new to Nelson. He attended his first meeting of the African National Congress (ANC) where he once again met Walter.

Nelson listened to the pleas of the black people of the country. He soon realised what the ANC was about and decided to join the organisation.

Every night Nelson attended meetings at different homes or halls. He listened to the speeches of people from all over the country as they spoke about the unfair white government destroying their lives and making them slaves.

Nelson returned home to his tin shack room after meetings. He would study until the early hours of morning. The words and happenings of the day would haunt him as he tried to fall asleep. He could still hear the cries of the nation, "Why must we as African people take an Africans Only bus, go to an Africans Only school, stay in an Africans Only township, be born in an Africans Only hospital and be laid to rest in an Africans Only grave? Why can't we share?"

"Why do we have to work in the white people's homes, offices, mines and on their farms? We get paid almost nothing and are treated with no respect." Nelson would drift off into a deep sleep with the words still ringing in his ears. In the morning, he would rise to witness and experience his people's lives of insults and humiliation at the hands of the white government.

As Nelson made his way to work in his old and over-patched suit, he knew he had to educate himself to fight the white government. These thoughts surrounded him every day as he walked six miles to work through Alexandria township and saw the needs of his people.

After returning home one night Nelson found a message under his door. It was addressed to Madiba, which was Nelson's clan name, telling him that the regent was in the city and wanted to see him.

Nelson was happy to see the regent again. Although he was nervous, he tried to look his best. Not once did the regent mention or ask about why Nelson and Justice had run away.

"Madiba," said the regent, "I am getting old. I need Justice at home. Please help me convince him to come home." Alas, Justice would not hear of it. He was determined to stay and work in the city. The regent left, heartbroken.

Six months later Nelson received word of the regent's death. He was shocked and sad. He travelled back to the Transkei with Justice to attend the regent's funeral. Upon arrival they discovered they had missed the burial. Nelson was glad to be back home. He was more overjoyed when Justice decided to stay and not to return to the city. Justice succeeded to his father's throne as the new regent. After spending a few days at the palace and visiting his mother at Qunu, Nelson returned to Johannesburg. He continued his studies and his fight in the struggle for freedom.

Nelson's hard work finally bore fruit. He passed his exams and received his degree at the university. He was surprised and pleased when the regent's wife and his mother attended the ceremony. Nelson was dressed in a new suit which was bought with money borrowed from Walter Sisulu.

More happy days were to follow. While visiting Walter and his wife Albertina, Nelson met his first wife-to-be, Evelyn. She was pretty, and Nelson's legs felt like jelly when he first saw her. Stuttering for the right words Nelson managed to ask her out on a date. After a few months he asked her to marry him. With little money in their pockets and lots of love in their hearts Nelson and Evelyn started a new life. They stayed with Evelyn's brother for a short while before getting a little place of their own.

Nelson returned home from work one night tired and hungry. Evelyn prepared a special meal for him. Nelson was worried that he may have forgotten an important date, as he searched his memory. The worried look on his face changed to a broad smile when Evelyn's sweet voice said, "Nelson, we are going to need a bigger house. I am going to have a baby." They found a bigger house at No. 8115 Orlando West.

As a family man, Nelson tried his best to keep Evelyn happy. Most days after work he attended the meetings of the ANC. He sometimes managed to slip away to the gym and box with his friends. This was a relief from all his daily duties. Although Nelson never had the chance to become a real boxer, he loved the sport. He would take his son along which gave Evelyn an opportunity to be by herself or to work on her nursing studies.

The marriage came under strain. Evelyn became tired of worrying about Nelson every night. His life was in constant danger at times. The police would break down the door in the middle of the night looking for Nelson or searching the house. At this point Nelson and Evelyn had been married for eleven years and had three children. Evelyn wished Nelson would leave the city and take his family back to the Transkei where he could open his own office as a lawyer. Nelson desperately tried to get his two sons interested in the struggle. He wished they would understand the white government's unfair treatment of the African people.

One night, Nelson returned home to find an empty house. He discovered that Evelyn had left him and taken everything. He threw himself down on the floor where he fell asleep. He felt confused and tired. He had just spent two weeks in jail and needed some peace and quiet.

Walter and Albertina Sisulu loved their close friends Nelson and Evelyn very much. They tried their best to get the marriage to work again, but there was nothing anyone could do. It was a very sad turn of events for everyone, and Nelson could see his own hurt in his children's eyes as well.

Nelson tried to put his life back together again. He hoped that one day his family would understand his predicament. The government was not making his life easier. He tried to defend his people in court as well as himself. Nelson and his partner Oliver Tambo had the first black law firm in the city and worked from their small offices there. They were threatened by the police who wanted them to move their business to a black area. They refused to do this as most of their clients worked in the city. The police sometimes walked into their offices and removed papers belonging to clients. These papers were never returned, leaving Nelson and Oliver very frustrated. Sometimes they lost clients to white companies.

At times, Nelson was not allowed to leave the city to defend his clients in other towns. Permission had to be granted by the magistrate. This was refused most times. Africans were not allowed on the street after 11 o'clock at night, and faced arrest and prosecution if they were not indoors.

One day, Nelson drove down the road in a thoughtful mood. A young beautiful woman standing at the side of the road caught his eye. Nelson wanted to turn back, but decided against it. She was so pretty that Nelson could not forget her face for days. He wondered if he should have turned back to offer her a lift.

Weeks had gone by when Nelson was called to Oliver's office. He was busy with two clients and introduced Nelson to them. It was as if someone had poured cold water over him. There she was, the young woman. Nelson had goose bumps as he took her hand. She was just as pretty as the day he saw her at the bus stop. He could not believe his eyes. His heart skipped and beat so hard he was almost sure everyone in the room could hear it. She introduced herself as Winnie Madikizela. She was the first black social worker at Baragwanath Hospital.

Nelson was in love again. He had met someone who believed in the fight against the white government. It was a match made in heaven. Winnie met his three children and loved them. Happy and full of smiles the days went by more easily. Winnie was understanding. They could sit at night and talk about the ANC and the people's struggle for hours. They were soon married. But again there was no time for a normal married life. The ANC took up more and more of Nelson's time.

Nelson would often travel to other cities to attend meetings with other members of the ANC. He spoke to people in the mines and became popular.

Nelson explained to people what to do and what not to do, should they come into conflict with the law. He would sometimes be followed by policemen and taken to jail, only to be sent home the next day.

After four years of defending and fighting an important court case, Nelson and his friends won what was called the Treason Trial. Thousands of Africans celebrated in the streets that day, singing *Nkosi Sikelel' iAfrika*. The white government was beaten at their own game.

Ten

Catch Mandela

Nelson wasted no time. He knew the government would send the police to arrest him after the court case. He went into hiding as soon as he left the court building, followed by his friends Oliver, Walter, Joe Slovo and many others who followed suit. Road blocks were set up all over the country. Nelson and his friends went to different regions of South Africa. Together they planned ANC strikes and marches in the dark hours of the morning. All this was done in utmost secrecy.

"If this white government will not listen to the people then we have to fight them with every weapon we have," Nelson said. Some members of the ANC decided a people's army was needed to defend the dignity of black people and to fight against the Apartheid government. A farm, Liliesleaf, was bought by white comrades who believed in the aims of the ANC. Strikes were planned from this hidden hideout. It became the headquarters of the newly-formed ANC army, better known as *Umkhonto we Sizwe*.

The struggle for freedom was intensifying. It was decided to bomb all government buildings at night when no people could get hurt. No lives were to be taken. Neither were white people the target of attacks. The aim of the sabotage was to get the government to start talking to the ANC.

Almost every day, the newspapers had stories about Nelson. Reporters started calling him the Black Pimpernel, after the Scarlet Pimpernel, a storybook character who was hard to find and catch during the French Revolution. They told the people of Nelson's daring actions in evading the police. The people loved it. Nelson became a hero and the newspapers made money.

Nelson missed his wife Winnie and their two daughters, Zinzi and Zenani, whom he hardly saw. Ahmed Kathrada would help at night moving Nelson from place to place. He would also help arrange secret visits with Winnie and the children. For this, Nelson was grateful and cherished these short and happy moments with his family. He knew that the police were watching Winnie, hoping she might lead them to him. These secret visits gave him strength to fight apartheid with all his might.

Nelson would sometimes wear a disguise. He dressed up as a gardener wearing blue overalls with a garden fork over his shoulder. He would pass his daughters' school during their lunch break just to see them playing with their friends then return to his hiding place.

Dressed as a driver, he sometimes drove past his house in the afternoon hoping to get a glimpse of Winnie. Nelson felt heartbroken to be hunted like a wild animal in his own country. He would sometimes be lucky and see her outside their home. On one such daring trip Nelson was stopped by a black policeman. As the perspiration ran down his forehead the policeman just smiled and winked at him. Relieved and knowing that the policeman knew who he was, Nelson continued on his way. He felt very happy to know that the ANC had members everywhere.

But inside the ANC there were also spies who reported everything to the government for money or favours from the police. To be as safe as possible, the method of contact between Nelson and Walter was kept a secret. Only certain members were trusted to carry messages. When one such message came, Nelson was prepared. He was to leave the country to be trained as a fighter in one of the African countries. The Government tried everything to stop him, but nothing was going to get in the way of the Black Pimpernel.

Nelson was invited to attend a meeting in Addis Ababa, capital city of Ethiopia, a country in north Africa. He grabbed this chance with both hands. Nelson knew that he could use this opportunity to get the ANC much needed help from other African countries. So he slipped out of the country to attend the meeting.

In the meanwhile, something happened about which Nelson knew nothing. His friend Walter had been arrested by the police. He had been on his way to bid Nelson farewell.

Eleven

The African journey

Crossing the South African border into Botswana proved easy. Nelson was nervous of being caught by the police. He was relieved when they reached the other side and happy to know he had entered a new country.

They made their way to the small town Lobatse. After staying there for nearly two weeks they finally boarded a small aeroplane and started their journey into Africa. They went on a second aeroplane journey to Mbeya, a town in Tanzania. Nelson was very frightened when they flew into a storm. The pilot frantically tried to make contact over the radio but had no success. Luckily the clouds cleared and a bright clear blue sky welcomed them as they flew over the beautiful jungle forest below.

Nelson knew what was expected of him. This was a very important trip and could be his last for a long time.

For the first time he met a black leader of an African country. He was amazed to see whites working for black people. When he heard a white lady call her boss "Sir", Nelson shook his head. He thought of his own country, South Africa. "If only our people could live like this. Then I wouldn't be here today asking for guns and money to fight a white people's police."

Sudan was the country where Nelson met his old friend Oliver Tambo, whom he had not seen for two years. Oliver was living in London after he was forced to flee South Africa. After a warm hug Nelson knew Oliver was glad to see him again. They talked until the early hours of the morning. Nelson told Oliver about the ANC back home.

It became time to make their final trip to Addis Ababa. During this part of the journey, Nelson found another old friend. It was Gaur, who had first taken him to an ANC meeting, when he started his first job in Johannesburg. While meeting so many friendly and known faces, Nelson realised how many people, black and white, were forced to leave their own country.

A big meeting attended by people from all over Africa took place. It was the biggest ever of its kind. Nelson was prepared as he had gone to ask for help in the fight for freedom for all South Africans. His aim was to tell the rest of the world what and who the ANC was. Nelson thought it was an honour to stand before so many important people. He received cheers and applause after he addressed the leaders.

Nelson left for Egypt after the meetings to fulfil a lifelong dream. He visited the pyramids and crossed the river Nile, the longest river in Africa. Looking at these wonders of the world, Nelson thought of his country and the way the white people treated Africans without any respect. Yet it was the African who made the first paper, counted in numbers, built the pyramids and made the calendar to count the days, months and years while the white man was still living in caves eating raw meat.

After a short visit to London, Nelson returned to Ethiopia to be trained as a soldier and commander for the new ANC army called MK.

Twelve

Return of the
Black Pimpernel

Nelson trained as a soldier in a
small army camp in Addis Ababa.
He enjoyed the exercise very
much because of his training
as a boxer. Nelson learnt to use
different guns. At night he
studied about how to lead an
army on a battle field.

Nelson received a telegram one
morning urging him to return
home as soon as possible to lead
MK against the white government.

The newspapers spread the news
of Nelson's return, weeks before
his actual arrival. The people were
delighted, but not the police. Every
policeman all over the country was
on the lookout for Nelson. Many
people were questioned and jailed,
including Winnie and her family.
The police hoped to obtain
information about Nelson's
whereabouts in this way.

Nelson slipped cautiously into the country. He was glad to be back. He was met by a friend, Cecil. They headed back to the secret safe house at Liliesleaf farm in Rivonia. This was where Nelson stayed before his African journey.

Walter Sisulu, Joe Slovo and other top ANC members held meetings with Nelson. He told them about his journey, the military training he had undergone and his meetings with the leaders of other countries. Excited and overjoyed at the success of the trip they talked until the early hours of the morning.

Nelson dressed in his blue overalls met other labourers during the day. He did not want to attract any attention to himself. Unlike in the city, Winnie and the children could at least visit him. When no one was around they took long walks on the farm together.

Planned meetings with other members of the ANC took place almost every night behind closed doors. Nelson started to train his small army in what was called guerrilla warfare. Their aim was to blow up any unguarded government building. These plans made the police angry. It scared the white government as they tried everything in their power to catch Nelson.

On a cool and clear winter's day Nelson and Cecil travelled back to Liliesleaf after attending meetings in Durban. They were overtaken by another car and forced off the road. Within seconds they were surrounded by policemen who asked them their names and what their business was in the area. Nelson gave his false name, David. "We know who you are, Nelson Mandela and we've got you," said the one policeman.

Driving back with the police Nelson realised how wide a net had been cast for his capture as he listened to the police radio in the car. "Remove all road blocks and return to your stations, Mandela is caught," a voice crackled over the air in triumph. Hiding his gun and a small notebook under the seat Nelson remained relaxed. He was disappointed that he had not been extra careful. He knew his freedom was to be taken away for a long time. Once again his family would suffer.

Thirteen

Living in jail

In Johannesburg they were taken to jail. Nelson was locked in a single cell, away from Cecil. While settling down for the long night ahead, Nelson suddenly heard a familiar cough coming from one of the other cells. "Walter, is that you?" Nelson called.

After a short silence, a surprised reply came. "Nelson, I don't believe they caught you. Yes, it is me, Walter." They continued their conversation until late. They were happy to have found one another although they were both in jail.

The newspapers were having a field day. The story of the Black Pimpernel was on every front page. All over the world, people were following it. Nelson and his friends were seen as heroes. As the days went by, more and more ANC members were arrested. The entire country came to a near standstill as the white government started to flex its muscles.

Being a lawyer, Nelson could start to prepare his case defending himself. He had chosen Joe Slovo, another lawyer, to help and advise him. Joe was one of the white people that had seen the wrongs of the government, and had chosen to fight them.

Nelson knew what he was up against, and expected a short jail sentence. The trial had lasted many months and it was finally time for the verdict. A deathly silence fell over the court room as the verdict was read out. "Nelson Mandela, you will serve five years in jail, for planning strikes and leaving the country without a passport."

Nelson turned to his supporters, raised his clenched fist and shouted, "Amandla! Amandla! Amandla!" Hundreds of supporters, inside and outside the court building, burst into song singing *Nkosi Sikelel' iAfrika*. Then Nelson was led away.

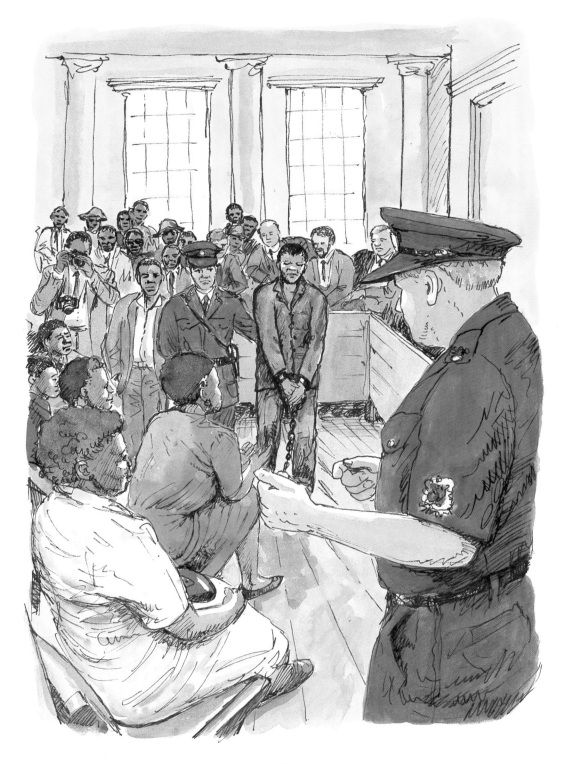

After a few weeks he was loaded into a police truck with other prisoners and taken to Cape Town. While they drove through the night Nelson wondered about their destination. Before they left, one of the policemen told him, "You are going to like your walks on the beach, Mandela." Nelson and his comrades were going to Robben Island.

The Cape Town docks crawled with police when the prisoners arrived. A ferry took them across the small stretch of ocean separating the island from the mainland. To be in jail is not fun, Nelson thought, as they were told to strip naked. Their clothes were thrown in cold water. Afterwards they were told to put them back on.

At times, the warders were like animals. They shouted at Nelson and his friends, "Here you are all going to die. This is the island."

The days as an imprisoned freedom fighter were long and hard. "This is all part of fighting the enemy," Nelson kept saying to himself. He tried to get by one day at a time. Even in prison Apartheid was enforced as blacks got less food than coloured and Indian prisoners. The food was horrible. Sometimes rice water was served as the only meal to prisoners who stepped out of line. This was water left from the other prisoners' rice and served cold in dirty buckets.

The days became weeks. The weeks became months. Nelson was slowly beginning to adapt to prison life. After spending a long day in the quarry chopping up stones, Nelson was told to get ready to leave. Not knowing what to expect he obediently did as he was told.

They left early the next morning heading back to Pretoria. At least in Pretoria prison he could get some news about his friends and Winnie. He knew something was wrong when he heard that his comrade Harold Wolpe was also in jail. Nelson was worried. He knew the government was planning something big. One morning as he walked along the corridor he got a fright when he saw a familiar face. It was the foreman of Liliesleaf farm. Nelson greeted him as he passed. The blood rushed to Nelson's head and his heart was beating so loud he was afraid someone might hear it. "The police has discovered the farm," he thought out loud.

Nelson was called to the office a day later only to find the rest of the group already there. Walter Sisulu, Ahmed Kathrada, Govan Mbeki and other top leaders in the ANC were charged with bombing and wanting to destroy the white government. This was the famous Rivonia trial that helped to paralyse the ANC. The police thought they had destroyed the ANC.

The court case was long and tiring. Almost nine months after the arrest of the accused the government finally won their long-awaited victory. Nelson and his friends were found guilty. The ANC had many important friends all around the world. The South African government felt threatened from all sides. Instead of passing down the death sentence, Nelson and his co-accused were sentenced to life in prison.

Nelson took one last look at Winnie, who sat next to his mother in the packed court. He gave her a smile knowing he might never be a free man again. Winnie tried to smile, although her heart was breaking. She waved goodbye with a clenched fist.

It was almost midnight when they finally stopped singing freedom songs. The prison became quiet. Nelson stared at the ceiling thinking of the many moments he would not share with his family. He was told by the prison warder to pack his things.

Outside in the courtyard they were given sandwiches and cold drinks. "You are going to the seaside, Mandela," said a prison warder. Nelson knew what it meant. The other prisoners did not like the news but were excited to learn that they would board an aeroplane.

Nelson preferred to travel in a police truck. An old Dakota army aeroplane was used to fly them to Cape Town. The ice cold wind blew through every possible opening. Their thin prison clothes offered no protection at all. They finally reached Cape Town.

The Rivonia trialists flew over the little matchbox houses of the Cape Flats. It was a pretty view with Table Mountain guarding the beautiful city. The city awoke to another cold winter's day as the aeroplane descended. It landed on the far corner of Robben Island.

Still shackled together they were taken to the prison building. Everyone was stripped and searched. They were given new khaki prison clothes. Nelson noticed that all the African prisoners were given short pants while the rest got long trousers. Not wanting to make trouble on the first day, he left it at that.

Over the years Nelson became a respected prisoner amongst his fellow inmates. As he had led and helped his people outside the prison, he continued to do so behind bars. He always took time to build a relationship with each prison commander and warders. He showed respect to everyone. Gaining respect was not always easy. Whenever Nelson became too friendly with a prison commander, the government became uneasy. They would replace the commander when this happened.

Nelson made time to study between his work duties. He would encourage young men to do the same. Although prison life was hard at times, one should prepare for a better life when freedom would eventually knock on the door. Like his father, Nelson strongly believed in learning and fighting the white government with your tongue and knowledge.

Nelson helped other prisoners. He would smuggle advice to prisoners on how to get books to study in prison. He was always watched and it sometimes landed him in trouble with the prison guards. Punishment could be harsh as he found out many a times when he was left in a cell alone for days, with little food, if any.

Three months had passed before Nelson received his first visit from his wife Winnie. It was a moment to look forward to but he soon discovered the cruelty of his captors. Nelson was led into a small room, where he was seated in front of a small window with Winnie on the opposite side. Only her face was visible and the glass was very dirty.

Two years passed before Winnie was allowed another visit. Like the other helpless prisoners, Nelson could do nothing but accept this.

Sometimes prison life had its good moments. Nelson and his fellow prisoners worked on the beach pulling seaweed from the ocean. The ice cold waves lashed against their soaked bodies. They rewarded themselves by catching some crayfish and mussels. The guards were only too happy to help them stew this tasty dish in drums on the beach. They would all share in the day's

catch. Even the prison commander joined them once. It was during times like these that Nelson missed his freedom.

Nelson heard from people on the outside that the country was filled with resistance. The young students started to fight the white government. This news was brought to him by young men who should have been in school but became new prisoners on the island.

A visit Nelson treasured most was when his mother came to see him. "Madiba, are you well?" she asked. "You look very thin to me." Nelson tried to look his best, but he could not fool his mother. He could see the sadness in her eyes. Like all visits it was too short. When she left, Nelson felt sad. He would have loved to hug her, just that once. She died a few weeks later. She was gone forever. She must have come to greet me for the last time, Nelson thought as he held the telegram in his hand.

It was only a few months later when another telegram was sent to Nelson. This time it was his eldest son who had died in a car accident in the Transkei. Once again the prison refused to let Nelson attend the funeral. Thinking of the few sweet and happy memories, Nelson kept back the tears and sadness as Walter tried to comfort him.

Eighteen years passed. One day Nelson and three others were told to pack their belongings. No reason was given, but as a prisoner Nelson was used to this. It was only as they reached the mainland that one of the warders told him of their new destination, namely Pollsmoor Prison.

After an hour's drive through the city and into the plush area of Tokai they entered the main gates of this huge prison. It looked like an army camp at night. Without saying a word to one another they were ushered into a big cell where they were the only prisoners on the third floor.

The prisoners received more up-to-date news. Nelson was allowed to have a garden on the balcony outside his cell. The food was better and even the visiting area was modern. Nelson missed the island but would not trade it for the new-found luxuries of Pollsmoor.

When Winnie came to visit Nelson he was given the greatest surprise. When the warder fetched him for his visit Nelson was taken to a separate room. This was not the normal glass-caged room. It was in fact the contact visit room. For the first time in nearly twenty years Nelson could touch and hold Winnie in his arms.

Nelson knew it was time to talk with the government. The country was sinking deeper into violence. There was unrest and the killing of unarmed school children by the police and army. South Africa was fast becoming a killing field with a bleak future. The white government tried to hold on to power. This led to more offers of freedom being made to Nelson. However, he knew better and politely turned them down.

Nelson decided he should meet with President P.W. Botha. He explained to his ANC partners that the time had come to talk or lose the country to fire and war. "Our children are dying out there while we are rotting away in jail."

Fourteen

Freedom at the door

Nelson sent a message to the ANC in Lusaka. He told his old friend Oliver Tambo of his actions to start talks with the white government. He knew what to expect when the warders had a new suit made for him. Nelson was to meet some important people and had to be properly dressed.

Nelson was moved to a separate cell, away from Walter and his friends. They objected, but Nelson was happy as he knew the government wanted him to be alone to start the talks.

A group of government officials was formed to hold secret meetings with Nelson. Pulling no punches he explained what the ANC stood for and why they chose to fight the government. Nelson told them the history of the ANC: why and when it was started. Much to Nelson's surprise he discovered they had no idea of the true belief of the ANC and its people.

Sitting in his cell one day, a friendly warder who saw to Nelson's needs came into his cell. "Mandela, would you like to go for a drive in the city?" Nelson was startled but eagerly said yes. He took his first of many freedom rides.

They drove around looking at people doing their daily work. Nelson longed for his own freedom but knew it still was not possible. At a small café in a white area the warder stopped the car, and asked Nelson if he would like a cold drink. It was rather warm in Cape Town. Nelson said yes. Without any fuss the warden went into the shop leaving Nelson unguarded in the car. This was the longest wait for Nelson ever as he realised he could escape. Feeling very hot and with his heart beating hard

Nelson knew escape would ruin all his talks and he would once again be the Black Pimpernel. "No, if I leave jail it will be as a free man," he said to himself as the warder returned with the ice-cold cooldrinks.

Nelson experienced pains in his chest and was sent to hospital. The cold cells were the cause of the pain, said the doctor. After a small operation he spent almost six weeks recovering. Nelson enjoyed the attention of the nurses and doctors. After the operation, he did not return to Pollsmoor Prison. Instead, he was transferred to Victor Verster, in the winelands of the Cape.

A prison is not the word for this place, Nelson thought as he surveyed his new jail. A house on the prison ground with a pool and new electrical items was his new cell. He even had a cook to prepare his meals. Meetings took place here at all hours of the day. Nelson could smell victory and see his freedom.

Nelson was introduced to a further taste of freedom. He was allowed to entertain his family on his birthday. He listened to the delightful sounds of his grandchildren who had come to visit him.

Nelson had his first meeting with President P.W. Botha. The meeting went well. Nelson once again made his request clear to President Botha who did not put any demands to Nelson. They parted on a pleasant note. Nelson thought they had much to think about.

A month after their meeting President Botha resigned. The talks between Nelson and the white government continued as Nelson met the new president, F.W. de Klerk, at Tuynhuis in Cape Town. He set his demands to President de Klerk.

It was no surprise to him when all his demands were met. All non-violent freedom fighters were set free and the ANC was unbanned. Oliver Tambo and many others could come back home. South Africa was on its way to a new beginning. After twenty-seven years, Nelson Mandela walked out of prison a free man, but only after freeing his people first.

The world stood still on that day as planeloads of people came to see with their own eyes the release of the Black Pimpernel. Nelson was met by a sea of people as he held on to Winnie's hand. He spoke to his people on Cape Town's Grand Parade. "Madiba! Madiba!" chanted the people.

Nelson could only get to his home two days later. He slept under his own roof at 8115 Orlando West with hundreds of well-wishers singing with joy throughout the night. He remembered how he had looked forward to being alone with his family. That was impossible as Nelson spent the next months travelling the world. He was invited by leaders of many other countries.

In New York he was given a hero's welcome as ticker tape was dropped from the tall buildings by thousands of Americans. When visiting Britain, Queen Elizabeth II rolled out the red carpet to welcome Nelson.

At Goose Bay, a small Canadian airport north of the Arctic Circle, they stopped to refuel the plane. Nelson got out to stretch his legs. It was freezing cold outside. Noticing some people watching the aeroplane Nelson decided to have a closer look after he heard they were Inuits (American Eskimos). As Nelson came close they raised their clenched fists shouting, "Viva ANC!" They had come especially to see him on his brief stop. The air was less cold now as Nelson realised how small the world had become.

It took the ANC and the government four more years of speaking across the table to secure a free country. In the meanwhile, fighting still raged in parts of South Africa, as people showed their hatred for each other.

At his home in Qunu, Nelson received the news of the death of Chris Hani, a popular and respected MK commander. Nelson was saddened. The country was on the brink of civil war and Nelson pleaded with the people to stay calm. While still mourning the death of Hani, Nelson was dealt another blow. His long time friend Oliver Tambo died after a long illness. It was sad day for Nelson as he laid his friend to rest.

Fifteen

The President

Nelson cast his vote in KwaZulu-Natal during the election on 27 April 1994. He chose the polling station at Ohlange High School in Inanda, north of Durban. This was where John Dube, the first president of the ANC, was buried. For the first time Nelson felt truly free as he stood beside the grave. He knew the circle had been completed.

The ANC won the elections. Leaders from all over the world came to wish Nelson well at his inauguration ceremony.

Nelson Mandela stood on the steps of the Union Buildings in Pretoria while thousands of people celebrated on the lawns below. His thoughts at that moment went to those not present who had given their lives for the struggle. He thought of his mother and father. A tear of joy and happiness rolled down his cheek as he spoke to the new rainbow nation.

The bright blue African sky filled with jet aeroplanes and helicopters flew over saluting their new president.

President Nelson Rolihlahla Mandela spoke these words:

"Never, never and never again shall it be that this beautiful land will again experience the oppression of one by the other. The sun shall never set on so glorious a human achievement. Let freedom reign. God bless Africa."

Nelson Mandela
CHILDREN'S FUND

"Children are the future of our nation and as such they deserve all our love and care. They need to be nurtured in such a way that we strengthen the capacity of each young person to engage positively and successfully in every aspect of life."

President Nelson R. Mandela

With this thought in mind our President created the Nelson Mandela Children's Fund (NMCF) and promised to give one-third of his salary to it each year for five years.

The NMCF aspires to play a key role in changing the way children are treated and in helping with projects for our young people, particularly those who are:

- homeless, abandoned or abused
- disabled
- without a proper education because of poor past schooling
- at risk of habitual delinquency and in need of life skills, education and training so that they can find jobs
- in need of places to play in safety
- requiring disaster relief

In the first two-and-a-half years, the NMCF has invested a total of R13 538 million to benefit disadvantaged young people through 704 different projects in communities throughout South Africa.

Donors to the Nelson Mandela Children's Fund come from all parts of South Africa and from countries throughout the world. Children are also helping the President to raise money for the NMCF by collecting coins in bottles or jars and arranging fund-raisers such as art exhibitions, fashion shows, fun-runs, sponsored walks and 'civvies days' at their schools. Children's choirs have also been good at collecting funds during special concerts

President Mandela is a special South African who is a great leader and a much-admired statesman. We hope that you enjoyed reading about his childhood and his long journey to achieve real freedom, especially in the knowledge that by purchasing this book your family or friends have helped the President to assist children in our country who are in need.

THIS IS TO CERTIFY THAT I

....

AS A RAINBOW CHILD PROMISE TO

MAKE MY PARENTS PROUD OF ME

ASK GOD FOR DAILY GUIDANCE

DEPEND ON MYSELF

INSPIRE MY FELLOW BEINGS

BE AN EXAMPLE TO THOSE AROUND ME

AVAIL MYSELF TO THE NEEDS OF THE DESTITUTE

SIGNED BY ....

DATE ....